What's awake?

Barn Owls

Patricia Whitehouse

www.raintreepublishers.co.uk
Visit our website to find out
more information about
Raintree books.

To order:
☎ Phone 0845 6044371
▤ Fax +44 (0) 1865 312263
⊠ Email myorders@raintreepublishers.co.uk

Customers from outside the UK please telephone +44 1865 312262

Raintree is an imprint of Capstone Global
Library Limited, a company incorporated in
England and Wales having its registered office
at 7 Pilgrim Street, London, EC4V 6LB –
Registered company number: 6695582

Editorial: Nick Hunter and Diyan Leake
Design: Sue Emerson (HL-US) and Joanna
Sapwell (www.tipani.co.uk)
Picture Research: Susana Darwin (HL-US) and
Maria Joannou
Production: Jonathan Smith

Originated by Dot Gradations
Printed in China

ISBN 978 1 844 21358 0   (paperback)
15 14
14 13 12

**British Library Cataloguing in Publication
Data**
Whitehouse, Patricia
Barn Owls
598.9'7
A full catalogue record for this book is available
from the British Library.

Acknowledgements
The publishers would like to thank the
following for permission to reproduce
photographs: Animals Animals pp. 12 (J & B
Photographers), 19 (A. Shay); Corbis pp. 15 (Roger
Tidman), 23 (vole, Roger Tidman); David Liebman p.
16 (Roger Rageot); DRK Photo p. 11 (Andy Rouse);
Heinemann Library p. 23 (nest, Sue Emerson); Photo
Researchers, Inc. pp. 5 (Stephen J. Krasemann), 6 (Tim
Davis), 10 (Stephen Dalton), 13 (Stephen Dalton), 14
(Stephen Dalton), 21 (Jeff Lepore), 22 (Stephen
Dalton), 23 (feathers, Stephen Dalton; nocturnal, E. R.
Degginger; talons, Stephen Dalton), back cover
(feathers, talons, Stephen Dalton); PhotoEdit, Inc. p.
17 (Michael Newman); Visuals Unlimited pp. 4 (Steve
Strickland), 7 (Joe McDonald), 8 (W. Banaszewski), 9
(Jack & Nora Bowers), 18 (Robert Barber), 20 (S.
Maslowski), 24 (W. Banaszewski).

Cover photograph of a barn owl, reproduced
with permission of Animals Animals (J &
Photographers).

Every effort has been made to contact copyright
holders of any material reproduced in this
book. Any omissions will be rectified in
subsequent printings if notice is given to the
publishers.

CAUTION: Remind children that it is not a good idea to handle wild animals. Children should wash
their hands with soap and water after they touch any animal.

Some words are shown in bold, **like this.** You can find
them in the glossary on page 23.

Contents

What's awake?

Some animals are awake when you go to sleep.

Animals that stay awake at night are **nocturnal**.

Barn owls are awake at night.

What are barn owls?

wing

Barn owls are birds.

Birds have **feathers** and wings.

egg

Birds lay eggs.

Baby birds come out of the eggs.

What do barn owls look like?

Barn owls have white **feathers** on their faces.

Their other feathers can be grey or brown.

beaks

talons

Barn owls have short, sharp **beaks.**

They have sharp **talons.**

Where do barn owls live?

Barn owls live in dark places.

They build **nests** in caves or holes in trees.

They build nests in barns.

They build nests in piles of hay, too.

What do barn owls do at night?

Barn owls look for food.

They fly over fields.

Barn owls find something to eat.

They grab it with their **talons.**

What do barn owls eat?

Barn owls eat small **nocturnal** animals.

Barn owls eat mice.

Barn owls also eat **voles**.

A vole looks like a mouse with
a short tail.

What do barn owls sound like?

Barn owls make a loud hissing noise.

They do not hoot like other owls.

A barn owl's call might wake you
up at night.

How are barn owls special?

A barn owl can turn its head to see what is behind it.

It can hear very well, too.

A barn owl can hear better than
it sees.

It uses its hearing to find food.

Where do barn owls go during the day?

In the morning, barn owls go back to their **nest**.

They sleep until it is dark again.

Barn owl map

wings

talons

beak

Glossary

beak
sharp nose and mouth of a bird

feather
one of the light, fluffy things that birds
have all over their body

nest
place where a bird rests and lays eggs

nocturnal
awake at night

talons
sharp curved toes on a bird's feet

vole
small animal like a mouse with
a short tail

Index